FORT WORTH PUBLIC LIBRARY

3 1668 04316 1998

W9-AHA-952

CHILDREN 92 HAMLIN 2008
Dayton, Connor
Denny Hamlin

10/27/2014

NASCAR Champions

DENNY HAMLIN

Connor Dayton

FORT WORTH LIBRARY

PowerKiDS press.

New York

Published in 2008 by The Rosen Publishing Group, Inc.
29 East 21st Street, New York, NY 10010

Copyright © 2008 by The Rosen Publishing Group, Inc.

All rights reserved. No part of this book may be reproduced in any form without permission in writing from the publisher, except by a reviewer.

First Edition

Editor: Jennifer Way
Book Design: Michael J. Flynn
Layout Design: Kate Laczynski
Photo Researcher: Nicole Pristash

Photo Credits: All images © Getty Images.

Library of Congress Cataloging-in-Publication Data

Dayton, Connor.
  Denny Hamlin / Connor Dayton. — 1st ed.
      p. cm. — (NASCAR champions)
  Includes index.
  ISBN-13: 978-1-4042-3814-5 (library binding)
  ISBN-10: 1-4042-3814-X (libray binding)
  1. Hamlin, Denny, 1980– —Juvenile literature. 2. Stock car drivers—United States—Biography—Juvenile literature.
I. Title.
  GV1032.H24D39 2008
  796.72092—dc22
  [B]
                                    2007001216

Manufactured in the United States of America

Contents

Denny Hamlin is a NASCAR driver. He was born on November 18, 1980, in Chesterfield, Virginia. He now lives in Davidson, North Carolina.

4

5

Denny Hamlin has been a NASCAR fan since he was a young boy. He began racing when he was seven years old!

6

Denny Hamlin began racing in both the Craftsman Truck and the Busch **series** of NASCAR races in 2004.

8

Hamlin's first full year racing in the Busch Series was in 2005. He did very well, finishing in fifth place for the **season**.

Denny Hamlin did so well in the Busch Series that he moved up to the Nextel Series in 2005. This is the top NASCAR series.

When Denny Hamlin began racing in the Nextel Series, he decided to keep racing in Busch Series races.

15

Denny Hamlin's race number is 11. His car is a Chevrolet that is **sponsored** by FedEx.

The year 2006 was a great year for Denny Hamlin. He even won that season's **Rookie** of the Year **award** in the Nextel Series.

When he is not racing, Denny Hamlin likes meeting his fans. Driving is Hamlin's biggest interest. He is always looking for ways to remain a top NASCAR driver.

Glossary

award (uh-WORD) A special honor given to someone.

rookie (RU-kee) A new player or driver.

season (SEE-zun) The group of games or races for a year.

series (SIR-eez) A group of races.

sponsored (SPON-serd) Paid for by a person or company.

Books and Web Sites

Books

Eagen, Rachel. *NASCAR (Automania!)*. New York: Crabtree Publishing Company, 2006.

Schaefer, Adam R. *The Daytona 500 (Edge Books NASCAR Racing)*. Mankato, MN: Capstone Press, 2006.

Web Sites

Due to the changing nature of Internet links, the Rosen Publishing Group, Inc., has developed an online list of Web sites related to the subject of this book. This site is updated regularly. Please use this link to access the list: www.powerkidslinks.com/nas/dham/

23

Index

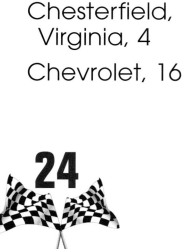